W9-CKE-754

Instant

Bible Lessons

Talking to God

by Pamela J. Kuhn

Rainbow Publishers

Rainbow Publishers • P.O. Box 261129 • San Diego, CA 92196

Dedicated to...

My sister, Melodie, and my soul friend, Shannon. Thanks for letting me brainstorm on your time (via fiber optics). Though you were many miles away, I could feel your prayers coming through the line to enlighten and energize my tired brain during computer shut-down.

INSTANT BIBLE LESSONS: TALKING TO GOD
©1998 by Rainbow Publishers, second printing
ISBN 1-885358-27-X

Rainbow Publishers
P.O. Box 261129
San Diego, CA 92196

Publisher: Arthur L. Miley
Illustrators: Roger Johnson, Joel Ryan
Editor: Christy Allen
Cover Design: Stray Cat Studio, San Diego, CA

Printed in the United States of America

Contents

Introduction

Do you want prayer to become an important part of your students' lives? If your answer is "yes," and I know it is, *Talking to God* is the book for you! With this book, you will introduce your students to Jesus' example in prayer, a consistent daily talk with God. Watch prayer become exciting for your class as they don their "robes" and listen to the story of the prodigal son, play a game of verse badminton or become involved in a skit. *Talking to God* contains dozens of activities to encourage prayer. Each of the first eight chapters includes a Bible story, memory verse and numerous activities to help reinforce the truth in the lesson. An additional chapter contains miscellaneous projects that can be used anytime throughout the study. Teacher aids are also sprinkled throughout the book, including bulletin board ideas and discussion starters.

As you work through the lessons, you may use your own judgment as to the appropriateness of the projects for your class. Everything in this book is designed to meet the 5 to 10 age range, however some activities may be more appealing to a younger group while others will more readily meet the abilities of older children.

The most exciting aspect of the *Instant Bible Lessons* series, which includes *God's Angels, Bible Truths* and *Virtues and Values* as well as *Talking to God,* is its flexibility. You can easily adapt these lessons to a Sunday School hour, a children's church service, a Wednesday night Bible study or home use. And, because there is a variety of reproducible ideas from which to choose (see below), you will enjoy creating a class session that is best for your group of students—whether large or small, beginning or advanced, active or studious. Plus, the intriguing topics will keep your kids coming back for more, week after week.

While I'm hoping this book will be a tool through which your class will learn, nothing takes the place of your own prayers for the students. As God blesses your innovative methods and the faithful teaching of your class, you can pray with Mary: "My soul glorifies the Lord and my spirit rejoices in God my Savior" (Luke 1:46-47).

How to Use This Book

Each chapter begins with a Bible story which you may read to your class, followed by discussion questions. Then, use any or all of the activities in the chapter to help drive home the message of that lesson. All of the activities are tagged with one of the icons below, so you can quickly flip through the chapter and select the projects you need. Simply cut off the teacher instructions on the pages and duplicate as desired. Also, see pages 87 and 88 for reproducible notes you can fill in and send home to parents.

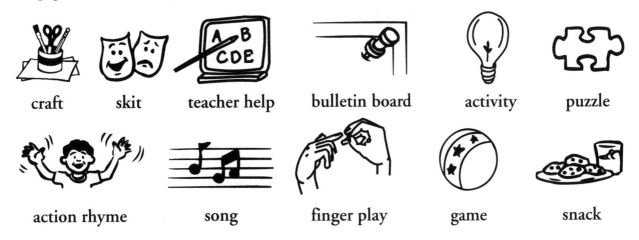

craft   skit   teacher help   bulletin board   activity   puzzle

action rhyme   song   finger play   game   snack

Chapter 1
God Hears My Prayers

Memory Verse

In the morning, O Lord, you hear my voice; in the morning I lay my requests before you and wait in expectation. Psalm 5:3

Story to Share
Jesus' Example

Jesus and four of His friends, Simon Peter, Andrew, James and John, were in Capernaum. It was the Sabbath so Jesus was teaching in the temple. The crowd was large because the people loved listening to Jesus teach.

Suddenly, a voice out of the crowd called out, "Let us alone! What do You want to do with us? I know who You are, You are Jesus of Nazareth, the Holy One of God!"

As the people looked around to see who it was, they saw a man with an evil spirit. Jesus did not even hesitate. He just spoke to the evil spirit. "Be quiet," He commanded. "Come out of him at once."

The man began to shake as the evil spirit, with a shriek, left him. The crowd was surprised. They had seen some of Jesus' miracles, but never before had they seen anyone with power to command evil spirits to depart.

Leaving the synagogue, Jesus went to the home of Simon and Andrew. Simon's mother-in-law was very ill with fever. Jesus gently reached for the sick woman's hand and lifted her up. Immediately, her fever left her and the family watched with joy as she helped prepare the meal for her guests.

Soon, others were coming to be healed. Crippled, blind, sick — they all came to see Jesus. Jesus loved helping people and spent a busy night healing.

How tired Jesus was! He slept only a few hours, though. There was something that was more important to Him than even sleep. Quietly, Jesus got up and made His way out of the city. He found a quiet place where He could be alone to talk with His Heavenly Father. He prayed for help and strength. God had given Him work to do and He needed help to carry it out.

Soon the disciples came looking for Jesus. Already people were wanting to be taught and healed. Now Jesus felt ready to give help where He was needed — He had talked to God.

— based on Mark 1:29-39

Questions for Discussion

1. Is morning the only time we should pray? What other times could we pray?
2. When do you like to pray?

Memory Verse Walk

Materials
•letters, duplicated
•scissors

Directions

1. Cut out the lettered squares and mix them up.
2. Line up the children in a straight line.
3. Without looking, choose a card.
4. Call out, "I am praying for someone with R." Everyone who has the letter R in their name takes one giant step forward and says the memory verse. Continue until all of the letters are used or one student reaches a designated finish line.

A	B	C	D	E
F	G	H	I	J
K	L	M	N	O
P	Q	R	S	T
U	V	W	X	Y
Z				

God Hears My Prayers

A Prayer for Me Each Day

song

A prayer for me each day,
A prayer for me each day,
Hallelujah, Praise the Lord,
A prayer for me each day.

Each day I pray for _____,
Each day I pray for _____,
Hallelujah, Praise the Lord,
Each day I pray for _____.

Directions

Sing to the tune of "The Farmer In The Dell." Select a child and form a circle around him or her. That child prays for someone in the room and that person joins him or her in the circle while the rest of the class skips around them. Continue until each child has been included in the middle. Note: If you notice one child is always picked last for games, let that child be "It" first so he or she may do the picking!

God Hears My Prayers

9

My Prayer Circle

craft

• • • • • • • • • • •

Materials
- circle patterns, duplicated
- black markers
- crayons
- pencils
- scissors
- paper fasteners

Directions
1. Have the students cut out the circles on the outer lines.
2. On the rim of the bottom circle, the children should write the names of eight people for whom they will pray.
3. In the pie sections, have them write for what they will be praying.
4. Allow the class to color the circles.
5. Show how to join the circles with a paper fastener in the center.
6. Show how to cut out the V section on the top circle.
7. Demonstrate how to move the circles.
8. Say, **As you pray, turn the dial and pray for someone different.**

My Prayer Circle

Selfish or Unselfish?

Jordon is having his prayer time.
Help him pray correctly by crossing out the selfish thoughts and drawing a heart around the good prayers.

Thank you for the sunshine.

Please give me a new ball glove like Mark's.

Mary is sick, help her feel better.

My sister needs new shoes. Help us know how to get them for her.

Help me be kind on the ball field.

<u>Show me what to do to help mother.</u>

Make our teacher sick so we won't have that test.

Thank you for helping me in Math class.

Solution is on page 96.

Materials
•activity, duplicated
•pencils

Discuss
Say, Should we always be asking God for things for ourselves? Such as: "Lord, I just have to have that new bike like Tommy's" or "Let me beat Carol in the race." Let's be careful that our prayers are unselfish. It is our privilege to pray. Let's keep selfishness out of them. And don't forget to thank God for what He has already done.

God Hears My Prayers

I Will, Too

Materials
- illustration, duplicated
- crayons
- scissors

Directions
1. Have the children color and cut out the picture on the outer solid lines.
2. Show how to fold the illustration on the dashed line, placing the children in the back and showing Jesus only.
3. Sing the song to the tune of "London Bridge Is Falling Down."
4. On the second verse, have everyone move the children flap forward.

Jesus prayed alone with God,
Alone with God,
Alone with God,
Jesus prayed alone with God,
I will, too!

I will pray every day,
Every day,
Every day,
I will pray every day,
Yes, I will!

God Hears My Prayers

12

Yep or Naw

Yep, That's true!

Naw, That's false!

Materials
•signs, duplicated

Directions
Duplicate (and enlarge, if possible) the cards at left to colored or heavy paper. Divide the class into two teams. Read the statements at the bottom left. Select a leader for each team to hold the team's sign when they stand. Switch sides halfway through so both groups can have a turn at each response.

Questions and Answers
1. Jesus and His friends were in New York City. *They were in Capernaum.*
2. Jesus was teaching in the temple. *true*
3. The crowd loved hearing Jesus teach. *true*
4. A pig came into the temple. *A man with an evil spirit was in the temple.*
5. Jesus told the evil spirit to "Be quiet, come out of him at once." *true*
6. The evil spirit told Jesus to sit down and be quiet. *The evil spirit obeyed Jesus.*
7. Jesus went to the home of the president. *He went to Simon and Andrew's.*
8. Simon's baby boy was sick. *His mother-in-law was sick.*
9. Jesus healed the sick woman. *true*
10. Jesus went to the doughnut store for breakfast. *He went out of the city to pray.*
11. Jesus needed to talk to God for strength. *true*
12. We should talk to God each day. *true*

God Hears My Prayers

Bible Food

snack

• • • • • • • • • •

Materials
- square, duplicated
- scissors
- glue or tape
- colored pencils
- whole dates filled with peanut butter
- powdered sugar
- waxed paper

Directions
1. Have the students cut out the square and make a cut at each corner's dashed lines.
2. Show how to pull each corner's two tabs on top of each other and glue or tape at each corner.
3. Allow the children to decorate their bowls using colored pencils.
4. Place a a square of waxed paper with powdered sugar on it in each child's bowl, and allow them to roll the peanut butter dates in the sugar, then eat them.

Discuss
Ask, What do you think Simon's mother-in-law served Jesus? It is very likely that they ate dates like these!

God Hears My Prayers

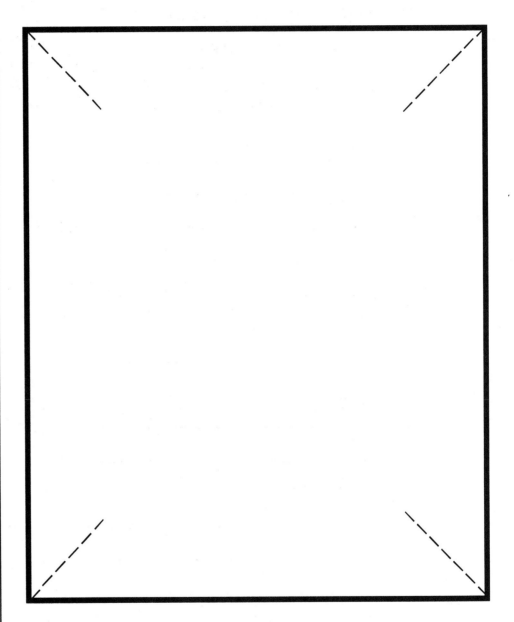

finished bowl

Capernaum Gazette

You are the reporter for the Capernaum Gazette.
Help write the front page of the newspaper.

TEMPLE NEWS
Evil spirit cast out by Jesus.
Simon's in-law healed of fever.
Jesus found praying.

activity

. . . .

Materials
•scroll, duplicated
•pencils

Directions
Duplicate the scroll newspaper and encourage the students to write their own descriptions of what happened in Capernaum. You may use the finished scrolls as a bulletin board or classroom wall display. If the students are willing, ask your pastor if they may read their "news" for the congregation.

God Hears My Prayers

Chapter 2
My Prayer of Confession

Memory Verse

I said, "I will confess my transgressions to the Lord" — and you forgave the guilt of my sin. Psalm 32:5

Story to Share
I Have Sinned

Jesus liked to tell stories called "parables." One day when a crowd gathered to hear Him teach, Jesus told them this parable: There was a rich farmer with two sons. One day the youngest son said, "Father, I know I will inherit part of your wealth when you die but I don't want to wait until then. Will you give me my portion now?"

The father agreed, and the young son took what was given to him and traveled to a far country. He lived extravagantly because he had lots of money to spend. He entertained his new friends in royal style.

Suddenly, to the son's surprise, the money was gone — and with his money went his friends. The son was left to beg for his food, but he could not find food or work. Eventually, a pig farmer hired him to watch over his pigs. The son was so hungry that even the pig food looked good to him.

As the son sat and watched the pigs eat, he thought, "Why am I here, starving, with no money, when my father has servants who are better clothed and fed than I? I'm going to go back to my father and beg him to forgive me. Surely he will allow me to be one of his servants."

So the son began the long journey back home. Soon he came into sight of his father's land. The son didn't know it, but the father had been watching for his son to come back home since the day he left. "He's here, my son who was lost is now found!" the father called out. He ran to meet his son, threw his arms around him and kissed him.

The son sobbed his confession: "Father, I have done a terrible thing to you and to God. I know I'm not worthy to be called your son. I will be honored if you would just accept me as one of your hired servants."

But the father was not angry. With a heart overflowing with forgiveness he said to his servants, "Bring the best robe to put on my son. Prepare a feast tonight. My son has come home!"

As Jesus was telling this story, He hoped the people would understand the lesson. God is willing to forgive anybody, as long as they are sorry for what they have done. Everyone who prays a prayer of confession can become a child of God. God is waiting for each of us to come to Him and will rejoice when we turn from our sin.

— based on Luke 15:11-24

Questions for Discussion

1. What is a prayer of confession?
2. Have you ever prayed this prayer? Would you like to now?

puzzle

Materials
•puzzle, duplicated
•pencils

Usage
All of the puzzles in this book are ideal for early arrivers to your class or as fill-ins for the extra few minutes you may have at the end of class. Have the puzzles duplicated and ready to distribute.

Missing Memory Verse

Fill in the missing words from the memory verse.
Use the word list to help you.

Then write the numbered letters in the blanks below
to see what kind of prayer you are praying.

forgave
confess
guilt
Lord
sin

I said, "I will __ __ __ __ __ __ __ my
          1   2 3   4

transgressions to the __ __ __ __ " — and you
                      5

__ __ __ __ __ __ the __ __ __ __ __
  6   7   8

of my __ __ __. Psalm 32:5
     9   10

PRAYER OF

__ __ __ __ __ __ __ __ __ __
1 5 10 3 7 9 4 8 6 2

Solution is on page 96.

All Gone

song
• • • • • • • • • • • •

Have you confessed all your sin, have you confessed?

Have you confessed all your sin, have you confessed?

Have you confessed all your sin?

Have you confessed all your sin?

Have you confessed all your sin, have you confessed?

Have you? (spoken)

Yes, my guilt of sin is gone, yes it is!

Yes, my guilt of sin is gone, yes it is!

Yes, my guilt of sin is gone.

Yes, my guilt of sin is gone.

Yes, my guilt of sin is gone, yes it is!

All gone! (spoken)

Directions

Sing to the tune of "She'll Be Comin' Round the Mountain." Have the boys sing the first verse to the girls. The girls respond by singing the second verse. Then the girls sing the first verse and the boys respond.

My Prayer of Confession

A Crowd of Listeners

craft

• • • • • • • • • • •

Materials
• large grocery sacks
• markers or crayons
• scissors

Directions
1. Say, **Our story to-day is about a crowd of people listening to Jesus tell a story. Let's get ready to be a part of that crowd.**
2. Show how to cut the sack according to the diagram.
3. Allow each child to color his or her "robe."
4. Dress the children in their robes and let them sit in a circle around you.

Variation
To add atmosphere to your story time, drape a large stool or chair with a brown or gray blanket for you to sit on and place large potted trees around the classroom.

My Prayer of Confession

cut down middle in back for easy on and off

head opening (cut circle and V-shape downward)

arm opening

Sinful Hearts

Draw a line from the story to the sin it describes.

1. Mary ran into the store for a gallon of milk. When the cashier turned his head, Mary put a candy bar in her pocket.

Cheating

2. Jamie spilled the paint and told the teacher Tyler did it.

Lying

3. Ben couldn't remember an answer on his science test. He looked at Emily's paper and wrote down her answer.

Disobedience

4. Amanda told the new girl her dress was ugly.

Stealing

5. "I'll never forgive you for this!" Anthony said when Justin broke his new arrow.

Unforgiveness

6. Heather's mother told her to come straight home from school, but Heather went skating instead.

Unkindness

activity
• • • • • • • • • • •

Materials
•activity, duplicated
•pencils

Directions
Distribute the sheets and allow the children to work individually on the matches. Then discuss the answers (on page 96) with the class. Ask the students to suggest other situations where they struggle with these sins in their lives.

My Prayer of Confession

Solution is on page 96.

craft

Materials
- wheels, duplicated
- crayons
- scissors
- paper fasteners

Directions
1. Have the students color and cut out the wheels.
2. Show how to place the "Prayer of Confession" wheel over the picture wheel and how to insert a paper fastener through the center.
3. Demonstrate how to turn the wheel to tell the story.

Discuss
Emphasize that the Story Wheel would be a good witnessing tool. Suggest to the students that they tell the story to a friend then ask, **Have you ever prayed a prayer of confession? Would you like to?**

My Prayer of Confession

Story Wheel

Prayer of Confession
Luke 15:11-24

Give Me My Money

**My little penny
was ugly,
until I made it gleam.**

**Just like my sinful,
black heart,
before Jesus
washed it clean.**

Materials
- bookmark, duplicated
- dirty pennies, one per child
- salt, two tablespoons
- white vinegar, six tablespoons
- basin of water
- towel
- glass jar
- measuring spoons

Directions
1. Say, **When the son got the money from his father it was shiny. But the newness wore off quickly. Let's see if we can get the shine back in these pennies.**
2. Pour the vinegar and salt into the jar.
3. As the students drop pennies into the jar, have them name sins God will forgive.
4. Leave the pennies in the jar about for five minutes while you join hands and thank God for forgiving our sins.
5. Allow the students to rinse and dry the pennies.
6. See craft at left.

My Prayer of Confession

Clean Heart Bookmark

Materials
- cleaned penny from activity
- bookmark, duplicated
- markers
- scissors
- glue

Directions
1. Have the students color and cut out the bookmark.
2. Show how to glue the penny to the middle of the heart.
3. Say, **Take your penny home to remind you that just like this penny was made clean, God makes our hearts clean by answering our prayers of confession.**

Leaving the Pigs

activity

Materials
- pigs, posts and pig pen, duplicated from pp. 24-25
- scissors
- glue
- crayons

Directions
1. Have the class color and cut out the pigs and fence posts.
2. Tell them they should glue the pigs in the correct order on the pig pen to say what the son said to the father in the lesson.
3. Then they should glue the fence posts in the correct order on the pigs to say what the father said to the son.
4. Say, **If you have told God you are sorry, write your name on the blank pig and glue it in the pen.**
5. Allow the children to finish coloring their pig pictures.

My Prayer of Confession

am

are

I

forgiven

sorry

You

Solution is on page 96.

I said, "I will confess my transgressions to the Lord"
— and you forgave the guilt of my sin.
Psalm 32:5

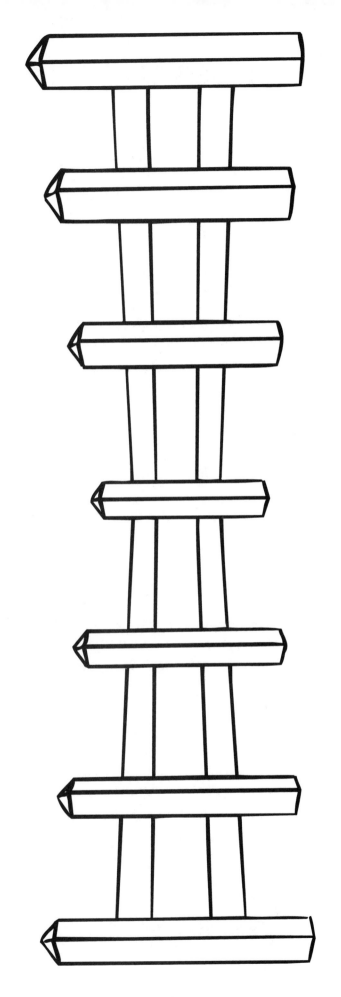

Chapter 3

My Prayer of Adoration

Memory Verse

I will praise you, O Lord, with all my heart. Psalm 9:1

Story to Share
Thank You, Jesus

Joab adjusted his hood and made sure his scarf was tight across his face. Why did he have to get this dreaded leprosy?

Joab didn't see Elias until he heard his excited voice. "Guess what?" he panted. "Jesus is coming this way today. My wife sent a messenger to tell me. This is the man who healed the sick and raised the dead. Surely He will heal us!"

Hope filled Joab's eyes as he looked around at the other nine men who were also lepers. Each of them had families they wanted to return to. Some of them had children, too. Joab had heard of this Jesus. He knew Jesus had performed many miracles; miracles only the true Son of God could perform.

That day as Jesus passed through the village, He heard, "Jesus! Jesus! Have mercy upon us!" Jesus turned and looked for who was calling Him. There in the distance were the lepers, not daring to come any closer to the road than the law allowed them to. "Jesus! Have mercy upon us," they cried again.

Jesus pointed back toward town. "Go and show yourselves to the priests," He said.

Joab and his friends didn't waste any time in obeying Jesus. They knew this was His way of saying, "You are healed!" because those healed of leprosy were to show themselves to a priest to live in town again.

All the way, Joab thought, "I'm healed. I can go to my wife and children. I can live in town. I am healed!" Then Joab remembered the One who restored his skin. Seeing the priest could wait; seeing his wife and children could wait. His heart was overflowing with thankfulness to Jesus, who had healed him.

Turning around, Joab ran back to Jesus. Falling at Jesus' feet, Joab bowed his head to the ground. "Thank You, Jesus, thank You!" he said as tears of joy and thankfulness fell from his eyes.

Jesus looked at Joab, and then He looked around. "But didn't I heal 10 lepers? Where are the other nine?" Then Jesus reached out and touched Joab. "By believing, you have become whole."

Jesus not only cured Joab of his leprosy, He also gave him a clean heart.

— based on Luke 17:11-19

Questions for Discussion

1. Adoration means to worship something. Why should we adore God?
2. Has He given you something that you need? Did you thank Him for His gift?

Praise Friends

game

• • • • • • • • • • •

Materials
• verse heart, duplicated
• scissors
• bag or sack

Directions
1. Cut out a heart for every two students.
2. Cut each heart in half, using a different line pattern.
3. Place the hearts in a bag and mix the pieces together.
4. Ask the children individually to share something for which they praise the Lord, then allow them to pick a heart half out of the bag. If odd number, teacher takes last one.
3. When everyone has a half, see who is able find their partner the fastest. Once matched, the partners must quote the memory verse to each other, then to the teacher together. The first pair back to their seats is the winner.

My Prayer of Adoration

"I WILL PRAISE YOU, O LORD, WITH ALL MY HEART."

PSALM 9:1

A Heart of Praise

craft

I will praise you, O Lord, with all my heart.

Psalm 9:1

finished craft

Materials
- patterns, duplicated
- markers
- scissors
- glue

Directions
1. Have the students cut out the hearts and arrows.
2. Tell them to write something they are thankful for on each arrow.
3. Show them how to glue the arrows around the verse heart as in the finished craft illustration.
4. Have each student write his or her first and last names on the small hearts and glue them to the bottom two arrows.

My Prayer of Adoration

Let's Praise God!

Directions

Sing to the tune of "This Old Man." You may bring in related props for the verses of this song and allow students to hold them up at the appropriate times. A wrapped gift, a piece of fruit, a ball cap, a pillow and an empty prescription bottle would work well, or be creative and come up with your own props.

Let's praise God! Let's praise God!
Let's praise God for His great gifts,
That He gives to show us His wondrous love.
Let's praise God together now!
Spoken: Thank You, God!

Let's praise God! Let's praise God!
Let's praise God for what we eat,
For bananas, pizza, cake and chocolate pie.
Let's praise God together now!
Spoken: Thank You, God!

Let's praise God! Let's praise God!
Let's praise God for what we wear,
For baseball caps, for our shirts and shoes,
Let's praise God together now!
Spoken: Thank You, God!

Let's praise God! Let's praise God!
Let's praise God for where we live,
For comfy homes with chairs and beds.
Let's praise God together now!
Spoken: Thank You, God!

Let's praise God! Let's praise God!
Let's praise God for our good friends,
For doctors, teachers, and Pastor _____,
Let's praise God together now!
Spoken: Thank You, God!

My Prayer of Adoration

Act It Out

One Comes Back

Cast

Jesus • Leper 1 • Leper 2 • Leper 3 • Leper 10 • extra lepers • extras for crowd

Script

Leper 1:   Hurry, hurry! I heard Jesus is coming this way.

Leper 2:   Maybe He will heal us.

Leper 3:   Here He comes now!

All lepers: *fold hands and bow, begging*
Jesus! Jesus! Have mercy on us!

Jesus: *holds up hand, points to town*
Go and show yourselves to the priests.

All lepers: *start back to town, hug each other, look at arms*
We are healed! We are healed!

Leper 10:   *stops, looks back, then runs back to Jesus, kneels*
Thank you, Jesus, thank You!

Jesus: Didn't I heal 10 lepers? Where are the nine? By giving thanks you have become whole.

Thankfulness Today

Cast

individual test takers • group of test takers • Jesus, voice only • teacher

Setting

Chairs set up like classroom.

Script

Test taker 1:   A math test today. Yuck!

Test taker 2:   I'm sure to fail it.

Test taker 3:   Me, too. I can never remember my multiplication tables.

Test taker 10:   I'm going to pray about it. Jesus can help us on our test.

Test takers 1-9: Yeah, that's a good idea. Let's pray about it.

Test takers 1-10: Please help us, Jesus. We need a good grade.

Teacher: These tests look great. I think all of you made As!

Test taker 4:   My mom will be so happy!

Test taker 5:   I am so happy!

Test taker 1-9: We are so happy. Let's go home. *leave*

Test taker 10:   *remains seated* Thank You, Jesus, for helping me take this test.

Jesus: Didn't I help the whole class? Where are the rest? Your thankfulness has made me happy.

Materials

•script, duplicated
•chairs

Directions

This page includes two skits you may use with this chapter's lesson. Many children love to act out what they are learning, so you may need to repeat the skits several times to allow them to take turns playing the various roles. Encourage them to put a lot of energy into their "performances" to make this activity fun.

My Prayer of Adoration

Vowels of Praise

puzzle

The vowels have been off praising the Lord

and didn't get back before we did the verse.

Can you fill in the correct vowels so we can read the verse?

__ w__ll pr__ __s__ y__ __, __ L__rd,

w__th __ll my h__ __rt. Ps__lm 9:1

Materials
•puzzle, duplicated
•pencils
•crayons

Directions
There are many ways to help children learn and memorize Bible verses, but puzzles are one of the most enjoyable methods. If desired, allow the children to color and take home this sheet as a reminder of this lesson's verse.

My Prayer

Write your own prayer to God.
If you have difficulty remembering to pray on a regular basis,
start writing your prayers to God each day in a notebook.
Then you can make sure you are praising Him!

activity

• • • • • • • • • • •

Materials

- frame, duplicated
- crayons
- pencils
- paper or construction paper
- glue

Directions

You may vary the way you lead this activity:

1. Duplicate the frame on white paper and have the students write their prayers in the middle, then color the frame. —or—

2. Duplicate the frame on white paper, then allow the students to glue it to construction paper. They may write their prayers on the construction paper and color the frame. —or—

3. Duplicate the frame on colored paper. The students may cut out the frame, glue it to white paper and write their prayers in the center.

My Prayer of Adoration

Thankful Heart

craft

• • • • • • • • • • • •

Materials
- patterns, duplicated from pp. 34-35
- scissors
- letter-sized envelopes
- construction paper
- crayons

Directions
1. Have the class glue the puzzle to construction paper for stability.
2. While the puzzle dries, have the students color and cut out the envelope decoration, then glue it to the front of an envelope.
3. Next, they should color and cut out the puzzle. Instruct the students to put the puzzle together and read the verse.
4. Have a race to see who can put it together fastest. Whoever finishes first should stand and say, "I have a thankful heart. I'm thankful for…"
5. Allow the students to take their puzzles home in the envelopes.

My Prayer of Adoration

"THIS PRAYER OF ADORATION BELONGS TO: _____ "

Chapter 4
My Prayer of Dedication

Memory Verse

Father...not my will, but yours be done. Luke 22:42

Story to Share
Your Will, Father

Jesus looked at the faces of His 12 disciples at this Last Supper. They had been His closest friends during His ministry on earth. Now His time was almost gone. Speaking kindly, with a trace of hurt in His voice, Jesus said, "One of you here will betray me."

The disciples couldn't believe it. Someone from among them would turn Jesus over to the enemy?

Jesus then broke the bread and handed it to His disciples: "Take this and eat it, may it remind you of my body." Then He blessed the wine and passed His cup: "This is to remind you of my blood."

After the disciples had eaten the bread and drank the wine, Jesus said, "This is what you should do to remember me."

The disciples had a lot to think about. They couldn't understand all Jesus was trying to tell them. They followed Jesus to the Mount of Olives. This quiet place, filled with beautiful old trees, was where Jesus needed to be. He needed to rest and think. He needed to pray to His Father.

"Stay here for a while," Jesus told the disciples. "I am going to pray." He took Peter, James and John with Him and went a little farther into the trees. "My heart is aching, My friends," He said. "Stay here and keep watch. I am going to talk to My Father."

Just a short distance from His disciples, Jesus fell to the ground. "Oh, Father. I know I am to die for the sins of wicked people. Is there any way I can escape the pain I am facing?"

As Jesus cried and prayed, the sweat poured down His face like drops of blood. "Father, isn't there any other way to save sinful men?" Finally, Jesus knew that God wanted Him to do this hard thing. "Yes, Father. I am willing to do what You ask Me to do. I want Your will."

With this prayer of dedication to God's will, Jesus arose and went to face His death on the cross. Whatever God wanted Him to do is what He wanted to do.

— based on Luke 22:39-42

Questions for Discussion

1. Have you ever prayed a prayer of dedication?
2. Would it be hard for you to give up your plans if that was what Jesus wanted you to do?

game

Materials
- squares, duplicated
- scissors
- tape
- recorded music and player
- bowl

Directions

1. Make two copies (enlarge, if possible) of the numbered squares and cut them apart.
2. Tape one set of squares to the floor in a circle.
3. Place the other set in a bowl.
4. Play music as the children walk along the numbered path. When the music stops, everyone should try to stand on a number.
5. Draw a number. The one standing on that number steps to the middle, kneels and says the memory verse. That child remains kneeling as you repeat the game.
6. Continue until everyone is kneeling.

My Prayer of Dedication

Follow the Path to the Mount of Olives

1	2	3	4	5
6	7	8	9	10
11	12	13	14	15
16	17	18	19	20

Prayer Mobile

My Prayer of Dedication

Your Will, Father

finished craft

Materials
- ring and Jesus, duplicated
- string
- crayons
- scissors
- tape

Directions
1. Have the class color and cut out the ring, its center and the Jesus figure.
2. Show how to cut a piece of string, tape one end to the Jesus figure, and the other end to the center of the circle on the back.
3. Allow the children to attach a second piece of string with tape for hanging.

My Prayer of Dedication

If It's Your Will

activity/song

Materials
- certificate, duplicated
- pencils
- heart stickers

Directions

Sing the song at top right to the tune of "Into My Heart." Sing it softly, then have them sign their name on the certificate, promising to do what God wants them to do. Stamp a heart on the card for the "seal." Post the cards where they can be seen to remind students of their promise.

If it's Your will,

If it's Your will,

If it's Your will, dear Jesus.

I'll gladly do what You want me to,

If it's Your will, dear Jesus.

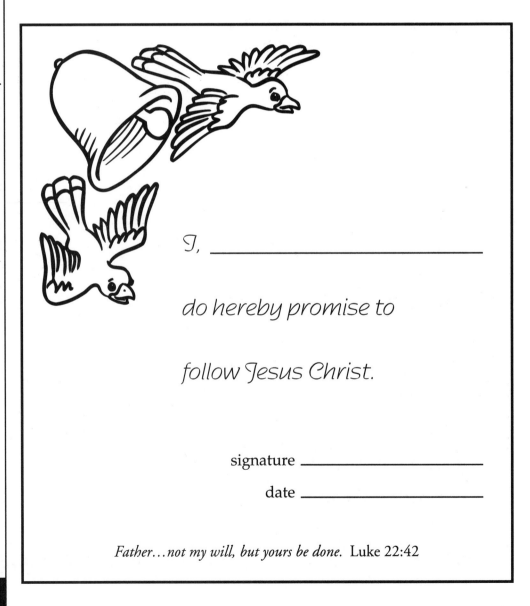

I, _____

do hereby promise to

follow Jesus Christ.

signature _____

date _____

Father…not my will, but yours be done. Luke 22:42

Look It Up

Turn to Luke 22:39-42 to fill in the blanks.
When you are finished, write the circled letters on the lines below to
find out who was praying a prayer of dedication.

Ⓐ__ __ __ __ went out as usual to the Mount of

__ __ __ __Ⓑ__ ,   and his __ __ __ __ __-

__ __ __Ⓒ__ followed him. He...knelt down and prayed,

"Father, if you are willing, take this __ Ⓓ__ from me; yet

not my will, but __ __ __ __Ⓔ be done."

__ __ __ __ __ __ __ __ __

Materials
•puzzle, duplicated
•pencils
•Bibles
•crayons

Directions
Younger students will need assistance in locating the verse in their Bibles. You could solve the puzzle together as a class, discussing the words that fit in the blanks and working through the letters for the blanks at the bottom. You may allow the children to color the illustration and take the page home as a reminder of the lesson's Bible story.

Solution is on page 96.

My Prayer of Dedication

Olive Trees

snack/activity

Materials
- olives
- toothpicks
- large dill pickles
- pepperoni slices
- waxed paper
- plastic knives

Directions

1. Give each child a square of waxed paper.
2. Show how to cut off the end of the pickle so it will stand.
3. Demonstrate how to spear the olives with the toothpicks and stick them in the pickle.
4. Allow everyone to make paths to their trees with pepperoni slices.
5. Eat and enjoy!

My Prayer of Dedication

Need something for early birds?

Try this...

Table of Interest

Gather the following items: communion set, grape juice, unleavened bread, large nail, crown of thorns (caution the children to be careful if handling the thorns), and Bible story books on the crucifixion of Jesus. Display everything on your classroom table. As the children arrive, allow them to browse through the items. Be available (or have a helper on hand) to answer any questions they may have. Insist on respect as the students handle the objects since they represent a solemn occasion. Later, use the items to lead the class in a discussion of communion. Children often have questions about the act of communion as they see it shared among adults in the worship service, so make this a safe and loving atmosphere for them to become involved in the communion experience.

Me

Each of us is different. We like to read different kinds of books, we like to eat different foods — even our hobbies are different from our friends. But guess what? God loves you. He made you. And He would like you to dedicate your likes and dislikes to Him. Fill in your answers, then sign your name on the last line.

My favorite color is _____.

I like to read _____.

My favorite food is _____.

I don't like to eat _____.

I like to study _____.

My hobby is _____.

When I grow up I want to be _____.

Here I am, Lord. You can have all of me. I say "YES" to your will for my life.

_____

activity

• • • • • • • • • •

Materials
•activity, duplicated
•pencils

Directions
Children love to express their individual preferences, and that act is even more special when they are told that God cares about their likes and dislikes. A fun variation of this activity is to make classwide versions using small notebooks or stapled sheets of paper. Each child writes a topic at the top of each of their pages—such as those at left—and makes the first page a numbered list. Then the children pass around their books. As each child fills out a friend's book, he signs in at a number in the front, then he writes his answer to the question on each page and writes his number below his answer. Your kids will enjoy leafing through their finished books to find out the preferences of their classmates and compare them to their own.

My Prayer of Dedication

Follow the Pattern

bulletin board

. . . .

Materials

- prayer and hands, duplicated from pp. 44 and 45
- lettering: Follow the Pattern
- lettering: And Your Life Will Turn Out Right.
- dress pattern and instruction sheet

Directions

1. Cover the bulletin board in the paper of your choice.
2. Place the lettering at the top and bottom center of the bulletin board, as shown in the finished illustration.
3. Post the dress pattern and instructions on the right of the board.
4. Attach the Lord's Prayer, slightly overlapping the dress pattern.
5. Post the praying hands on the left of the board.

Note: Lettering may be purchased ready to hang or cut freehand from colored paper. Dress patterns are available at fabric stores.

My Prayer of Dedication

finished bulletin board

Our Father which art in heaven, hallowed be thy name. Thy kingdom come. Thy will be done, in earth as it is in heaven. Give us this day our daily bread. And forgive us our debts, as we forgive our debtors. And lead us not into

Chapter 5
My Prayer of Direction

Memory Verse

For this God is our God for ever and ever; he will be our guide even to the end. Psalm 48:14

Story to Share
Show Me, Father

Jesus had a cousin, John the Baptist. God gave John the Baptist a special work to preach repentance to people. So John the Baptist wandered from place to place, preaching repentance. His coat was made from camel's hair and tied with a leather belt. He ate fat locusts and honey made by wild bees.

"Repent! Repent! Say you are sorry!" he urged. When they repented, John the Baptist baptized them. "I will baptize you with water," he said, "but Jesus is coming after me. He is such a pure man that I am not even worthy to unfasten His sandals. He will baptize you with the fire from the Holy Ghost."

One day as John was baptizing a group, he saw Jesus approaching. "Look," he cried, "here is Jesus, the Lamb of God, who will take away the sins of the world."

"John," said Jesus, "I want to be baptized."

As John baptized Jesus, the sky opened and the Holy Spirit took on the form of a dove, which hovered over Jesus. Then God spoke: "You are my Son, Jesus. I am pleased with you."

The people realized this was not an ordinary man. Large crowds began to come to hear Him teach about God. When they found out that He could heal the sick, they brought their family and friends to be healed.

It wasn't long before Jesus knew He needed some special friends who would be willing to leave their homes and travel with Him to help Him teach people about God.

Jesus knew this was a decision He couldn't make without His Father's help. He went to be alone and to pray for direction. "Father, show me the men you would have me choose," he prayed. "Help me to make the best choice."

Jesus prayed all night. When daylight came, Jesus knew who God wanted Him to appoint for His apostles. He chose Simon Peter, Andrew, James, John, Philip, Thomas, Matthew, another James, Thaddeus, Simon, Judas and Bartholomew. Jesus knew He had made the right choice because He had prayed for direction.

— based on Luke 6:12-16 and Matthew 3:13-17

Questions for Discussion
1. Have you ever prayed for God to show you what to do?
2. Are your friends pleasing to God?

game

Materials
- squares, duplicated
- scissors
- optional snacks

Directions
1. Cut apart the lettered squares and place them face down.
2. Have each child select and hold a square, then say the memory verse together. When a word is said that begins with a letter a child is holding, he "pops" or stands.
3. Start slowly, increasing in speed each time.

Variations
- Let the children watch popcorn pop so they will know how fast to "pop." Mix the popcorn with peanuts and candy-coated chocolate for a treat after they have played Popcorn Verse.

- Have the students write PRAY in large letters on construction paper. Allow them to glue popped popcorn on the letters. Let them take the posters home as a reminder to pray for direction.

My Prayer of Direction

Popcorn Verse

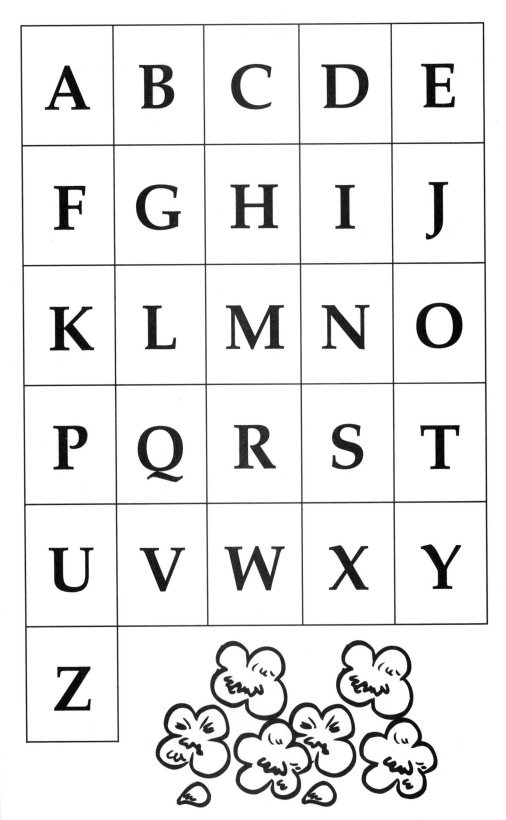

A	B	C	D	E
F	G	H	I	J
K	L	M	N	O
P	Q	R	S	T
U	V	W	X	Y
Z				

Steps of Guidance

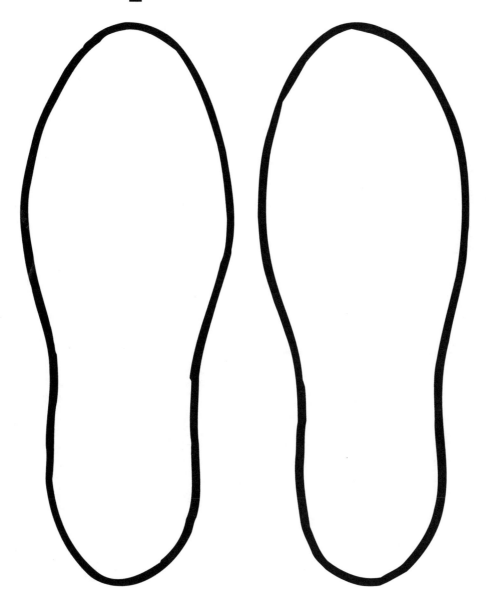

For this God is our God for ever and ever; he will be our guide even to the end.
Psalm 48:14

pendant

Materials
- footsteps and pendant, duplicated
- construction paper
- scissors
- hole punch
- yarn

Directions
1. Duplicate 10 sets of feet and cut them out.
2. Write a word from the memory verse on each foot.
3. Duplicate and cut out one foot pendant for each child.
4. Place the feet on the floor in a child's stepping distance.
5. Have the children take turns stepping from foot to foot as they say the memory verse together.
6. Give each child a foot pendant as they complete the course.
7. Allow them to punch a hole in it and string it with yarn for a necklace.

Variation
Make two sets of feet. and divide the class into teams. Each child steps on a foot and says the word. Have them increase their stepping speed for a challenge.

My Prayer of Direction

49

Following Jesus

When someone is guiding us, we follow wherever they go.
That's what we should do when Jesus is our guide.
If you follow Jesus through the maze below, He will guide you
right through the memory verse.

Materials
•puzzle, duplicated
•pencils

Directions
This puzzle is a good way for your younger readers to learn the memory verse. You may write the verse on the chalkboard to assist them in recognizing the words in the correct order. As each child finishes, have them individually read the verse to you from the maze to make certain that they understand it.

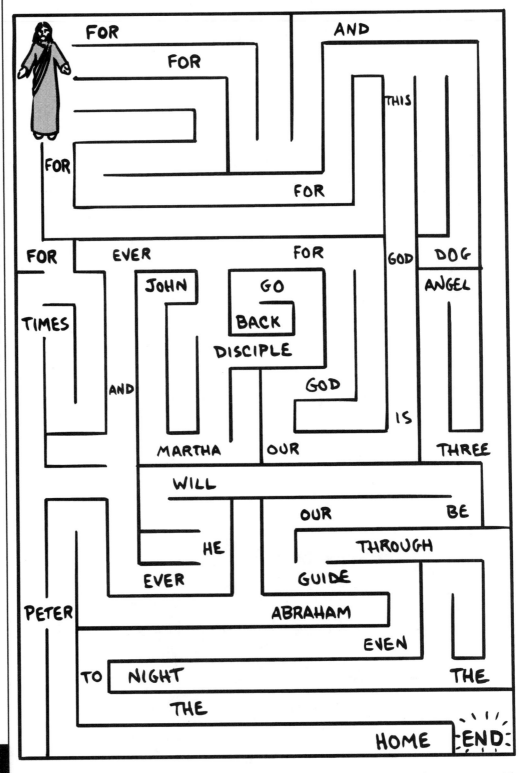

Friends!

Jesus prayed for God to help Him choose His friends. Have you prayed about your friends? Read the sentences below. If the person would be a good friend, circle the letter in the Yes row. If not, circle the letter in the No row. Then unscramble the letters to see who is our best friend and write it on the bottom lines.

puzzle

Materials
•puzzle, duplicated
•pencils

Usage
This puzzle could open a discussion of the importance of good friends. Relationships are an important issue to elementary-aged children as they begin to be confronted with peer pressure. Emphasize the value of Christian friends, but also encourage your class to be a "light" to non-Christians by showing them the ways of Jesus. Consider sharing a friendship story from your own experience that illustrates how we can show Jesus to others by our actions.

	YES	NO
Jane says, "I'm going to help Mrs. Baker rake leaves. Want to come help?"	S	P
Ryan says, "I like Sunday School, don't you?"	E	Q
Samantha says, "Let's not play with Anthony. He stinks!"	M	J
Jared says, "Let's play a game. You can be first."	S	G
Brooke says, "Let's go steal an apple off old Mr. Harold's tree."	B	U

Who is our best friend?

— — — — —

Solution is on page 96.

My Prayer of Direction

puzzle

Materials

•puzzle, duplicated
•pencils
•crayons

Directions

Even your youngest students are able to look for and count the doves in this illustration. Allow the children to color the picture after they have found the doves.

My Beloved Son

When Jesus was baptized, the Holy Spirit took on the form of a dove and descended down, hovering over Jesus. In the picture of John baptizing Jesus below, see if you can find 10 doves. Then color the picture.

For this God is our God for ever and ever;
he will be our guide even to the end.
Psalm 48:14

Prayer Stand-Up Reminder

craft

My Prayer of Direction

For this God is our God for ever and ever; he will be our guide even to the end. Psalm 48:14

shirt pattern

Materials
- figure, duplicated to heavy paper
- shirt pattern, duplicated
- crayons
- scissors
- flannel scraps

Directions
1. Have the students color and cut out the figure. Boys may cut off the ponytail to make their figure male.
2. Show how to place the pajama pattern on the flannel, trace and cut it out.
3. Have them glue the flannel to the figure.
4. Show how to fold the figure on the dashed lines so it will stand up.
5. Say, **Put your reminder next to your bed so you will remember to pray to God.**

My Prayer of Direction

Repent and Be Baptized

song

• • • • • • • • • • •

Directions

Sing to the tune of "Stop And Let Me Tell You." Props for this song could include water that you sprinkle on some students' heads for the first verse; a stuffed lamb toy for the second verse; and a Bible or a chart to point to the "list" on the fourth verse. For the third verse, have the students put an arm around a friend.

Repent! And say
you're sorry,
John the Baptist told them all.
Repent! And say you're sorry,
John the Baptist told them all.
With water I will baptize you,
Then Christ will come, the Savior true.
Repent! And say you're sorry,
John the Baptist told them all.

Look! The Lamb of God,
Who taketh away our sins.
Look! The Lamb of God,
Who taketh away our sins.
You are my Son, I am pleased with you,
The voice was heard from the sky so blue.
Look! The Lamb of God,
Who taketh away our sins.

God, give me direction,
In choosing my best friends.
God, give me direction,
In choosing my best friends.
Jesus prayed for God to help Him pick,
The twelve disciples who'd with Him stick.
God, give me direction,
In choosing my best friends.

God will help you, too,
When you pick your closest friends.
God will help you, too,
When you pick your closest friends.
He'll show you who will top the list,
Of those who will help you sin resist.
God will help you, too,
When you pick your closest friends.

Following Jesus' Instruction

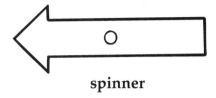

spinner

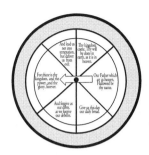

finished spinner

Materials
- spinner, duplicated
- 9" paper plates
- paper fasteners
- markers
- scissors

Directions
1. Have the students draw six sections on their plates by making an X then drawing a straight line through it, top to bottom.
2. They should write a part of The Lord's Prayer in each section (as listed at left).
3. Show how to cut out and attach the spinner in the center with a paper fastener.
4. Have the children spin their spinners. As you pray, they should say the phrase their spinner landed on with you. Everyone should say "Amen" together at the end.

My Prayer of Direction

The Lord's Prayer

(write one line on each section)

Our Father which art in heaven, Hallowed be thy name.
Thy kingdom come, Thy will be done in earth, as it is in heaven.
Give us this day our daily bread.
And forgive us our debts, as we forgive our debtors.
And lead us not into temptation, but deliver us from evil;
For thine is the kingdom, and the power, and the glory, forever.
Amen.

(adapted from Luke 11:2-4)

Discuss

Use this simple activity to help the children learn The Lord's Prayer. Most children will recognize the prayer but will not understand its meaning. Offer easy, memorable explanations for each line as you say it.

Chapter 6
My Prayer of Intercession

Memory Verse

Pray for each other. The prayer of a righteous man is powerful and effective. James 5:16

Story to Share
Mourning and Fasting

The Jews had been punished for their disobedience to God. King Nebuchadnezzar destroyed Jerusalem and carried most of the people far away to Babylon as captives. But when Cyrus was king of Persia he urged the Jews living in Babylon to go back to Jerusalem and rebuild the temple. He gave them all of the gold and silver that had been stolen from the temple by the Babylonians.

Now Artaxerxes was king. His cup bearer, Nehemiah, was a Jew. As cup bearer, Nehemiah had a place of honor in the king's service as the one who tasted the wine before the king drank it, to make sure it wasn't poisoned.

One day some Jewish men came to see the king. Always anxious for news from his home, Nehemiah asked the men about Jerusalem. "How is Jerusalem coming along?" he inquired. "Are the people still rebuilding?"

The men did not have good news for Nehemiah. "Jerusalem is in a terrible state," one said. "The walls of Jerusalem are broken and the gates are in ruins."

Nehemiah was heartbroken. He knew that without sturdy walls and gates the Jews would be easy prey for their enemies. For days, Nehemiah fasted and prayed: "Oh Lord God of heaven, the great and awesome God. Let Your ear be attentive to the prayers of Your servant. Prepare a way that I may speak with the king."

One day, while he was serving the king his wine, the king asked, "Nehemiah, what has made you so sad? Are you ill?"

"No," answered Nehemiah. "I am well, but my heart is breaking. I have heard news from Jerusalem that the walls and gates are in ruins. I beg you, release me from my duties here and allow me to return to Jerusalem so I may start the rebuilding."

"Nehemiah, you have been a good friend to me," responded the king. "I grant you your petition."

Nehemiah was overjoyed. He knew he had received God's answer to his fervent prayer.

— based on Nehemiah 1:3-11; 2:1-6

Questions for Discussion

1. A prayer of intercession means that we are asking God to help us, or intercede, in a situation. Are you praying about a special need?
2. Are you willing to give up candy or soda for a period of time to show God you are earnest?

Friendship Praying

puzzle

Melanie was praying for her friends and now she can't remember the memory verse. The names have the same number of letters as the words to the memory verse in the word list below. Fill in the correct words on the lines. A few hints are provided for you.

Jane Sue John Craig...Tom Joshua of a Elizabeth Abi is Leighton Kim Christina. Emily 5:16

P_____ _____ _____ _____. T_____

_____ of a _____ _____ is

_____ _____ _____.   _____ 5:16

Materials
•puzzle, duplicated
•pencils

Discuss
Say, **Do you pray for those in your class at school? Make a list of everyone in your class and pray for one each day of the week!**

Word List
prayer
righteous
pray
powerful
James
and
for
effective
each
man
other
the

My Prayer of Intercession

Solution is on page 96.

Nehemiah Changes Faces

craft/song

Nehemiah, Nehemiah

Crying, Crying, Nehemiah.
Weeping for Jerusalem.
He won't eat, but he will pray,
Will God's answer come today?

Happy, Happy, Nehemiah,
Has a smile upon his face.
Build your wall, the king did say,
Now Nehemiah's on his way.

Listen, Listen, to my story,
When you're earnest in your prayer,
God will give you what you need,
If to Him you humbly plead.

Materials
•Nehemiah faces, duplicated to heavy paper
•craft sticks
•glue
•scissors
•crayons

Directions
1. Have the children color and cut out the faces.
2. Show how to glue the faces to the craft sticks, back to back.
3. Lead the class in the song (to the tune of "Reuben, Reuben"), turning Nehemiah at the appropriate times.

Variation
If your copier has enlargment capabilities, make the faces bigger and glue them to paint stirrer sticks.

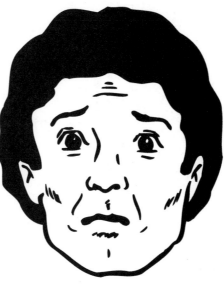

My Prayer of Intercession

Trouble in the Palace

Nehemiah is serving King Artaxerxes his wine.
But something is wrong.
Circle 10 things you think may be wrong.

puzzle

Materials
•puzzle, duplicated
•pencils
•crayons

Directions
Because they are often the recipient of corrections, children enjoy correcting others, even in a silly picture such as this. You may distribute the puzzle to the students for individual work or you can have the class call out the "mistakes" as they find them. Have the children explain their answers and discuss the differences in Bible times versus current day.

Solution is on page 96.

My Prayer of Intercession

60

Cupbearers

activity/snack

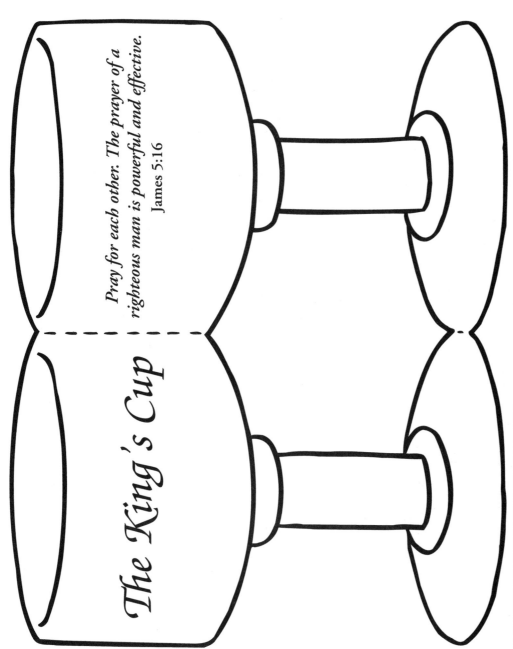

Pray for each other. The prayer of a righteous man is powerful and effective.
James 5:16

The King's Cup

Materials
- goblet, duplicated
- scissors
- glue
- stapler
- tape
- bathroom-sized cups
- white grape juice

Directions
1. Have the students color and cut out the goblet on the outer lines.
2. Show how to fold the goblet at the dashed lines and glue it together just at the stem.
3. Pass around a stapler and have the students staple the sides of the goblet. Cover staples with tape.
4. Show how to make a place for and set the foam cup inside the goblet.
5. Pour juice into their cups, then say, **Let's taste the juice to make sure it is fit for the king!**

My Prayer of Intercession

61

craft

Materials
- poster, duplicated
- old newspapers or magazines
- glue
- scissors

Directions
1. Have the children cut out letters from magazines or newspapers to spell the names of their friends.
2. Show how they should glue the letters to their posters.

Variation
Set a specific amount of time and see who can make the most names in the time allotted. No letters can be written — they must find them all in the magazines or newspapers.

My Prayer of Intercession

Prayer Poster

I am praying for...

Pray for each other. The prayer of a righteous man is powerful and effective.
James 5:16

I'm Praying for You

My Prayer List

_____

_____

_____

_____

_____

activity

• • • • • • • • • •

Materials
•prayer list and strip, duplicated
•markers
•ribbon
•scissors
•stickers

Directions
1. Have the students cut out the prayer list and the strip.
2. Lead the class in sharing prayer requests. Have the children write their requests on their lists. Pray for each need and encourage the children to pray.
3. Allow the children to write a message on and decorate the prayer strip, then show how to roll and tie the strip with ribbon.
4. Say, **Give your prayer scroll to someone you know who needs prayer and then remember to pray!**

I'm Praying for You

My Prayer of Intercession

63

Verse Badminton

game

Materials
- paper plates
- markers
- paint stirrers
- string
- balloons
- tape

Directions
1. Have the students write the memory verse on their plate.
2. Show how to tape a stirrer to the back of the paper plate to make a paddle.
3. Have the students find a partner, then tie string between two chairs to make a net for each team.
4. Allow the children to help you inflate the balloons.
5. Using the paddles, each team should volley the balloon over the string net. Each time they hit they should say a word of the memory verse.

Optional
Play with four people — two on each side of the net.

My Prayer of Intercession

64

Where Can I Pray?

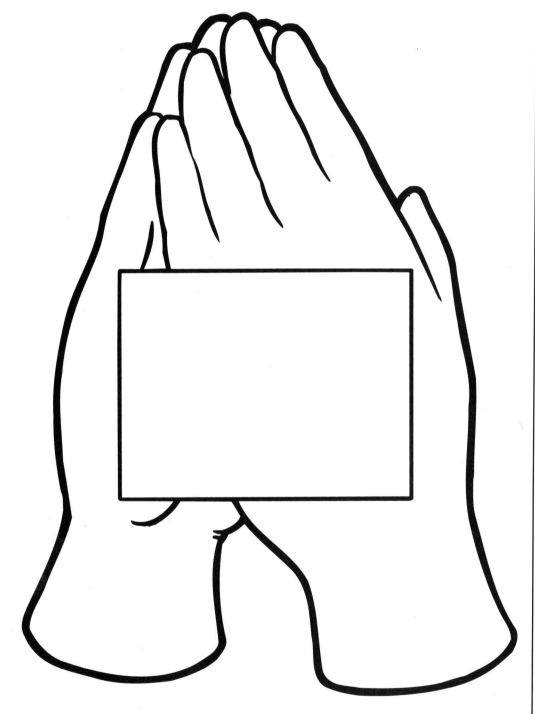

Chapter 7
My Prayer of Supplication

Memory Verse

Do not be anxious about anything, but in everything, by prayer and petition, with thanksgiving, present your requests to God. Philippians 4:6

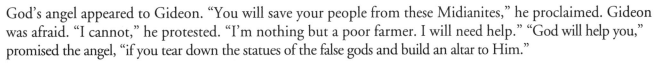

Story to Share
I Need Help, Lord

The Israelites were disobeying the true God by worshipping false gods. God allowed the Midianites to conquer them because of their sin. The Midianites stole the Israelites' animals and burned their food. Starving, the Israelites cried out to God. Even though they had been worshipping Baal, an idol, when they needed help they knew only the true God would hear them.

God's angel appeared to Gideon. "You will save your people from these Midianites," he proclaimed. Gideon was afraid. "I cannot," he protested. "I'm nothing but a poor farmer. I will need help." "God will help you," promised the angel, "if you tear down the statues of the false gods and build an altar to Him."

Gideon obeyed God. He and 10 servants smashed the false gods and built a new altar. Killing a bull they had brought with them, they burned it on the altar as an offering to the true God.

Gideon gathered together his army of 32,000. God had promised His help, but He wanted the Israelites to know it was God who helped them win the battle against the Midianites. "Gideon," God said, "you have too many soldiers. Tell the men who are afraid to leave and go home." Twenty-thousand returned home.

But there were still too many. "Gideon, take your men to the spring and watch how they drink," God commanded. "If they kneel and put their faces in the water, send them home. If they drink from their hands, they may stay and fight."

When those who put their faces in the water returned home, Gideon recounted his army. Only 300 men were left. But Gideon knew he had offered a prayer of supplication, a prayer for help.

Gideon waited until it was dark. Then he gave his men rams horn trumpets and flaming torches covered by earthenware jars. "When I give the signal, blow your trumpet, smash your jar to reveal your lighted torch, and shout 'The sword of the Lord and of Gideon,'" he commanded.

The army crept toward the army of Midian. When Gideon blew his trumpet, all 300 men blew their trumpets. They smashed their jars and their torches blinded the Midianites. Terrified and confused, the Midianites began fighting themselves and fled into the night. God had answered Gideon's prayer for help.

— based on Judges 6:11-27; 7:2-22

Questions for Discussion

1. Supplication means to ask earnestly and humbly for something. Can you pray a prayer of supplication?
2. Will God answer our prayers when have sin in our heart?

Talking to God

Prayer is just like talking to a friend on the telephone. You can't see your friend, but he hears you. You can't see God when you pray, but He can hear what you are saying. In the verse below, some of the letters have been left out. But don't worry, you have your telephone, so just punch in the numbers and see which letter you need to use to complete the verse.

Materials
•puzzle, duplicated
•pencils

Directions
Your older students will be able to do this puzzle on their own but younger children will need assistance. Help them select letters by sounding out each of the three options for each number and selecting the one that makes sense. Help the students memorize the verse once it is completed.

Do not be an___ious about an___thing, but in
　　　　　　　　9　　　　　　　　9

e___erything, by ___rayer and ___etition, with ___hanksgiving,
　　8　　　　　　　7　　　　　　7　　　　　　　　8

pre___ent your ___equests to ___ ___ ___.
　　7　　　　　　7　　　　　　　4　6　3

P___illip___ans 4:6
　　4　　　　4

Oops!
The Army Is Out of Order!

Oh my, what has happened? The story doesn't seem quite right! Number the sentences in order, then read the story to a friend to see if you got it right.

puzzle

• • • • • • • • • • •

_____Gideon gathered 22,000 men together and prepared to fight.

_____The Midianites were confused and fled into the night.

_____Gideon gave each man a ram's horn trumpet and a flaming torch covered by a jar.

_____Gideon burned an offering to God and prayed, "I need help, Lord."

_____Gideon sent his army home until only 300 men were left.

_____Gideon's men smashed the jars, blew the trumpets and shouted.

_____An angel told Gideon, "You have been chosen to save your people from the Midianites."

Now try this... Can you remember a time you prayed, "I need help, Lord?" Can you tell about it in four sentences? Mix them up and see if your friend can put them in order.

_____

_____

_____

_____

Materials
•puzzle, duplicated
•pencils

Directions
Use this puzzle with your older students who are able to sufficiently read and write. This is a good activity to encourage friendship and help new children get to know regular class attenders. To extend the puzzle, have the students exchange the puzzles they make with several classmates.

My Prayer of Supplication

Solution is on page 96.

Flag of Victory

snack

• • • • • • • • • •

Materials

- flag patterns, duplicated
- scissors
- crayons
- glue
- toothpicks
- fruit, bite-sized

Directions

1. Have the children color and cut out the flags.
2. Show how to fold a flag on the dashed line.
3. Instruct the children to place a toothpick inside the creased edge of the flag and glue the sides together.
4. Have them use the toothpick end to "spear" the fruit.

Discuss

Say, **Gideon won the battle. He could wave the flag of victory! His greatest weapon was prayer. If you pray, you can wave the flag of victory, too.**

My Prayer of Supplication

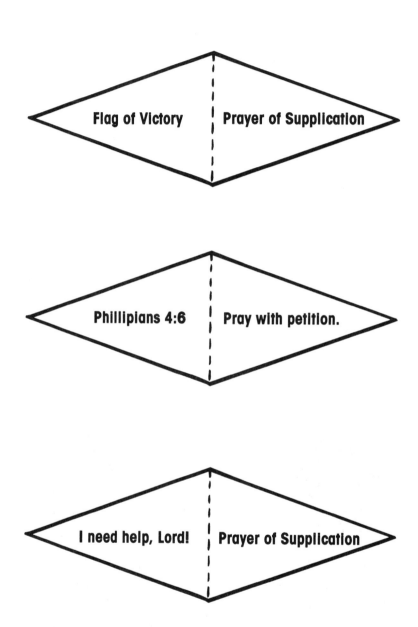

Jesus Hears Me

When we need help Jesus is always ready to hear our prayer.
Use the word list to finish these sentences about
Jesus hearing when you pray.

I can pray at work or _____ay.

I can pray both night and _____ay.

I can pray at home and _____ay.

When I pray, Jesus hears what I _____ay.

When I need help, I can _____ay.

<u>Word List</u>

pray

away

play

say

day

Materials
•puzzle, duplicated
•pencils

Directions
After the students finish the puzzle, have them sing the song with you to the tune of "Jesus Loves Me." Then pray with the children, emphasizing thanks that we may pray anywhere and at anytime and God hears us.

Jesus Hears Me

Jesus hears me when I pray,
If at night or in the day.
If I'm home or far away,
Jesus hears each thing I say.

Yes, Jesus hears me.
Yes, Jesus hears me.
Yes, Jesus hears me.
He hears me when I pray.

**My Prayer
of Supplication**

Our Battles

We may not have enemies like the Midianites, but we sure do have some battles to fight, don't we? Battles with our schoolwork, battles with keeping the right attitudes on the playground, battles wanting to obey our teachers and parents. What battle do you fight? Gideon told the Lord, "I need help." Why don't you tell Jesus you need help fighting your battle, too?

Materials
• letter, duplicated
• pencils

Directions
Explain that there are many ways we can pray to God — out loud, in our head, and in written words. Encourage the students to share their inner-most thoughts in the letter and allow a few moments for them to find a quiet space to write their prayers. Suggest that they keep the letter private be-tween them and God. Pray with the class at the end of the activity and ask God to be with the children as they fight their battles. Let them take their prayer letters home so they can continue to pray about the need.

```
            Dear Jesus,
  I have a battle I am fighting.
             It is

_____

_____

_____

_____


    I know you will help me,
  just like you helped Gideon.
    Thank You for Your help.
             Love,


    _____
```

Do not be anxious about anything, but in everything, by prayer and petition, with thanksgiving, present your requests to God.
Philippians 4:6

My Prayer of Supplication

Weapons

God told Gideon to use some unusual weapons to fight the Midianites. Find them below and circle them. God also gave us some special weapons to help us fight our spiritual battles. Find them and draw a box around them. Draw a smiling face on them if you have used them.

puzzle

Materials

- puzzle, duplicated
- pencils, markers or crayons

Directions

Explain to the class the difference between an actual battle like Gideon fought, and the spiritual battles that Christians face in the world. Then tie the two together by suggesting that just like God gave Gideon weapons to defeat the Midianites, He also gives Christians weapons to fight bad things in our lives. Ask for other ideas for how God helps us to defeat the enemy.

Solution is on page 96.

My Prayer of Supplication

craft

My Prayer Basket

Materials
- cards, basket and handle on pp. 74-75, duplicated to heavy paper
- Bibles
- glue or tape
- scissors
- pencils

Directions
1. Have the class cut out the prayer cards, basket and handle.
2. Show how to cut the basket on the dashed lines and fold and glue or tape the tabs together with the design on the outside to form the basket.
3. Have the students glue or tape on the handle.
4. Using their Bibles, they should look up the Bible verses at right and write them on the cards.
5. Say, **Put your cards in your basket and pick a card to read each day to remind you it is important to pray.**

My Prayer of Supplication

Ephesians 6:18	John 15:7
James 5:15	1 Timothy 2:8
Matthew 26:41	1 Thessalonians 5:17

prayer cards

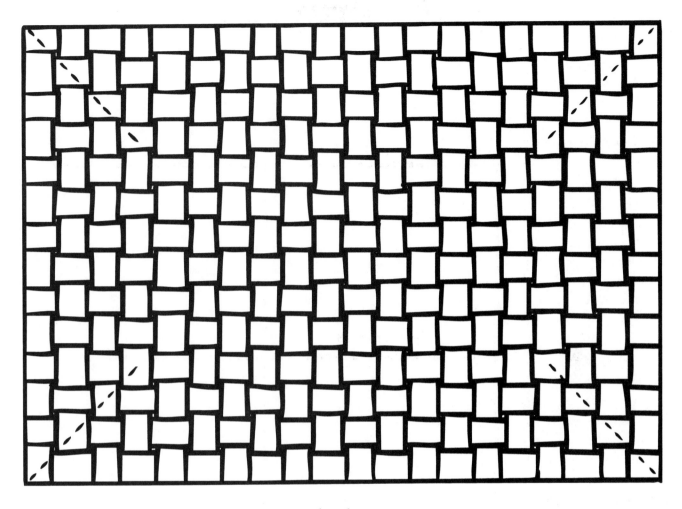

basket

handle

finished basket

Chapter 8
My Prayer of Determination

Memory Verse

Be joyful in hope, patient in affliction, faithful in prayer.
Romans 12:12

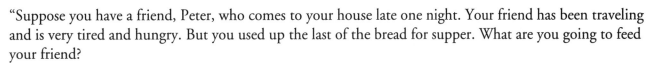

Story to Share
Persistence Works

Jesus loved to teach His disciples. He taught them to pray simple and sincere prayers. He also taught them to spend time alone talking to God.

Jesus was the greatest storyteller who ever lived. One day, when He was teaching His disciples how to pray, He told them this story:

"Suppose you have a friend, Peter, who comes to your house late one night. Your friend has been traveling and is very tired and hungry. But you used up the last of the bread for supper. What are you going to feed your friend?

"'I know,' you say to yourself, 'I will go to my friend John's house and ask him to lend me some bread.' Quickly, you make your way to John's house, eager to get some bread for this hungry traveler.

"You knock at the door and call, 'John, John, I need some bread.' John doesn't even get out of bed to come to the door. He just yells, 'My family and I are in bed. Please don't bother us.'

"'But John,' you protest, 'I have a friend at my house and nothing to feed him.'

"'Go away,' John yells. 'Come back when it is morning. I'm trying to sleep.'

"'No,' you answer. 'I am not going away without some bread. My friend is hungry and I need bread. Now!'

"John finally gets up and gives you a loaf of bread, and you hurry home to feed it to your friend. Just like this story, My disciples, so it is in prayer. Ask, and it will be given to you; seek and you will find; knock and the door will be opened to you."

The disciples all nodded their heads. They knew God would always give them what was best, even though it wasn't always what they wanted. Sometimes the answer would be "yes," sometimes "no," sometimes "wait." But the answer would come.

— based on Luke 11:5-10

Questions for Discussion
1. Do you have something you've been praying about for a long time?
2. Will God answer your prayer?

Begging for Bread

snack/game

• • • • • • • • • •

Materials
• recipe, duplicated
• 2 cups of peanut butter
• 1 cup of powdered sugar
• ½ cup of honey
• waxed paper
• damp washcloth for clean-up

Directions
1. Combine ingredients and mix well.
2. Give each child a piece of waxed paper and a mound of the play clay.
3. Say, **Make some "bread" so you will have enough if your neighbor comes to borrow.**
4. Allow the children to play-act borrowing bread from one another, then encourage everyone to eat their bread.
5. Distribute the recipe for students to make edible play clay at home.

My Prayer of Determination

Edible Play Clay

2 cups of peanut butter
1 cup of powdered sugar
1/2 cup of honey

Combine and mix well.

Be joyful in hope, patient in affliction, faithful in prayer.
Romans 12:12

Looking for a game?
Knock It Out!

Have everyone sit in a circle. Knock out the rhythm for a name. Whoever's name matches that rhythm stands and says the memory verse. For example: Em-i-ly (knock knock knock) or Da-vid (knock knock). After one round, the children may want to take turns knocking.

Memory Shapes

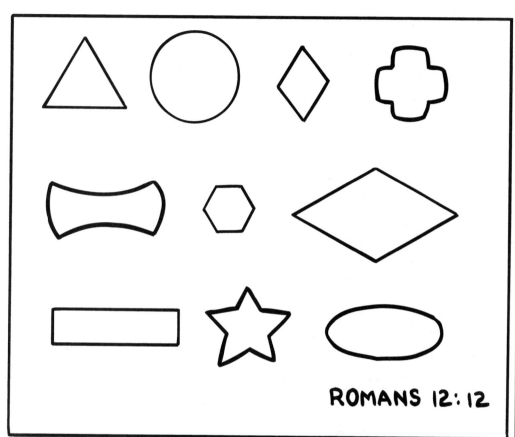

ROMANS 12:12

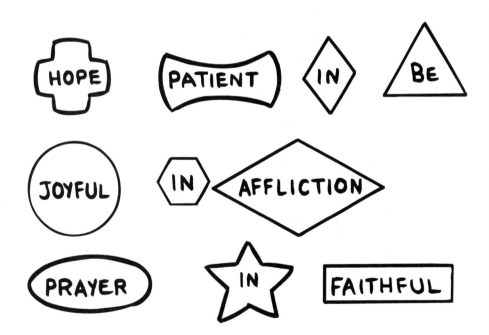

Materials
- puzzle board and pieces, duplicated
- scissors
- construction paper
- envelopes
- crayons

Directions
1. Have the children cut out and glue the puzzle board and pieces to construction paper.
2. While the glue dries, allow them to color the puzzle.
3. Have them cut out the puzzle board and pieces again.
4. Explain how to match the puzzle pieces to their correct shapes on the board to review the lesson's memory verse.
5. Give everyone an envelope to take home their puzzles and practice the verse again.

My Prayer of Determination

Solution is on page 96.

craft

Materials
- bright 9" x 12" foil gift wrap
- wrapped candies
- tape
- ribbon

Directions

1. Show how to roll together the long edges of the paper, overlapping them slightly, and tape without creasing the tube.
2. Pass around candy and allow the children to fill their tubes.
3. Demonstrate how to twist the ends of the tube and tie closed with ribbon.
4. Have the class split into pairs. Each pair should say the memory verse to each other, then each child should grab one end of the popper and pull.
5. After the poppers burst, have the children share their candy and their prayer requests with the group.

My Prayer of Determination

Persistent Poppers

Discuss

Say, **We need to be persistent in other areas of our lives besides prayer. Are you persistent in your schoolwork, or do you always turn your homework in half-finished? Are you persistent in practicing your musical instrument, or do you stumble through your piece when it's time for your lesson? What about chores you are given to do at home? When you and your partner pull the popper, you must be persistent to make it come apart. Let's be persistent in all of life!**

Determination Knock

Even though I'm smaller

crouch down to floor

Than my father and my mother.

stand and put hands over head

I can knock with determination.

knock on chair

Directions

Younger children especially enjoy action verses — and they can be a welcome break for those whose attention spans may be a little short. Demonstrate the words and movements for them several times. You will be surprised how quickly they catch on!

Again, and again, and again.

knock again and again

To him that knocks, the door will be opened!

knock, hold hands palms together then open

puzzle

- - - - - - - - - - -

Materials
- puzzle, duplicated
- pencils

Directions
After your class finishes the puzzle, ask what it means when we say that Jesus is the "Bread of Life." Discuss how we are fed by Jesus' love through His guidance and through the Bible, God's Word.

Bread, Please!

How many slices of bread are in your loaf?
Put a letter in each slice to fill up your bag.

Fqr ⬚⬚⬚⬚⬚⬚⬚ whq ⬚⬚⬚ receives; he whq ⬚⬚⬚⬚⬚ finds; and tq him whq ⬚⬚⬚⬚⬚, the ⬚⬚⬚ will be qpened. Luke 11:10

Something is still wrong.
The yeast must have been bad.
Try changing the q's to o's and see if your loaf looks any better.
Write the verse in the loaf below.

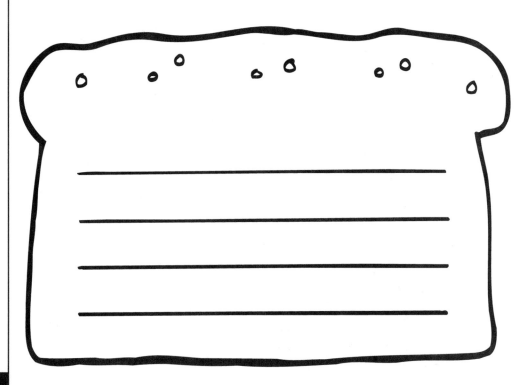

Solution is on page 96.

Go Away, I'm Sleeping

skit

Cast
father
mother
boy
girl
Mark
Peter

Props
loaf of bread
four blankets
chair

Materials
•script, duplicated
•loaf of bread
•four blankets
•chair

John
Script

Father, Mother, boy and girl are sleeping on two blankets with two blankets covering them. Peter is sitting in a chair.

Mark knocks near Peter's chair.

Peter *gets up and goes to door* Mark! Great to see you.

Mark *shakes Peter's hand vigorously* I thought I'd come and visit you for a few days.

Peter I'm glad you did. Come in and sit down. Are you hungry?

Mark I sure am! I could eat a cow.

Peter Well, I'll just run over to the Quick Mart and get some bread. I'll be right back.

    Peter throws up his hands. The Quick Mart is closed! Maybe John will have some bread. *knocks at John's door*

John Go away. We're sleeping.

Peter *knocks again* I need a loaf of bread.

John No way, come back tomorrow. *pulls blanket over his head*

Peter *knocks again, louder* I need a loaf of bread.

John You'll wake my kids and then you'll have to stay to babysit.

Peter *knocking again, still louder* I need a loaf of bread now!

John *takes the bread to Peter* Oh, here. Now go away!

Peter Yes! For everyone who asks receives; he who seeks finds; and to him who knocks, the door will be opened.

Directions
Kids love to act out what they have learned. Select your better readers for the vocal roles and allow your quieter students to participate through non-speaking parts.

My Prayer of Determination

My Friends and I

craft/skit

• • • • • • • • • •

Materials

- finger puppets, duplicated
- crayons
- tape
- scissors

Directions

1. Have the children color and cut out the puppets on page 85.
2. Show how to tape the puppets around your fingers—Jesus on one hand, the Bible times people on the others. Small children may tape a figure around several fingers or even their wrists.
3. Read the skit aloud as the children use their puppets. Then sing the song at the bottom to the tune of "Mary Had a Little Lamb."

My Prayer of Determination

Skit

Said one of Jesus' disciples, "If you've got time today,

Come and teach my dear friends just how we should pray."

Jesus nodded his head and said, "Yes, I will.

Sit here around Me and be very still.

Our Father which art in heaven, Hallowed be thy name.

Thy kingdom come, Thy will be done in earth, as it is in heaven.

Give us this day our daily bread.

And forgive us our debts, as we forgive our debtors.

And lead us not into temptation, but deliver us from evil;

For thine is the kingdom, and the power, and the glory, for ever. Amen."

Jesus Showed Me

Jesus showed me how to pray,

How to pray, how to pray.

Jesus showed me how to pray,

I will pray each day.

Chapter 9
Miscellaneous Projects of Prayer

Dear Parent,

We sure have had fun learning about PRAYER!

This is what we studied:

_____

_____

Thank you for praying for us each week.

_____
teacher

teacher help

Directions

Duplicate and distribute the note. Check off the items you need and insert the date on the blank line when you want them brought in. You may issue one note at the beginning of the eight lessons or issue one note per week or every few weeks, depending on your needs.

Help!

Dear Parents and Friends,

We are learning about talking to God. There are a lot of items we need for upcoming lessons on the importance of prayer. Could you help by sending in any of the following on _____ ?

❑ balloons
❑ blankets
❑ candy, wrapped
❑ craft sticks
❑ cups, bathroom-sized
❑ dates, whole
❑ dill pickles, large
❑ envelopes, letter-sized
❑ flannel scraps
❑ fruit, bite-sized
❑ gift wrap, bright foil
❑ grape juice, white
❑ grocery bags, paper
❑ honey
❑ newspapers or magazines, old
❑ olives

❑ paint stirrers
❑ paper fasteners
❑ paper plates, 9"
❑ peanut butter
❑ pepperoni slices
❑ photo of your child, small
❑ plastic knives
❑ powdered sugar
❑ ribbon
❑ self-stick plastic, clear
❑ stickers, Bible themes
❑ string
❑ toothpicks
❑ waxed paper
❑ yarn

Thank you!

_____
teacher

My Prayer Markers

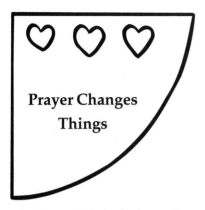

Prayer Changes Things

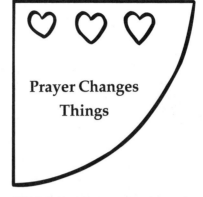

Prayer Changes Things

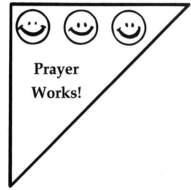

Prayer Works!

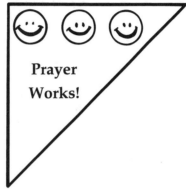

Prayer Works!

God Answers Prayer!

God Answers Prayer!

Prayer Is… Talking to God!

Prayer Is… Talking to God!

craft

Materials
- Bible markers, duplicated
- letter-sized envelopes
- scissors
- markers
- glue
- Bibles

Directions
1. Have the class color and cut out the markers.
2. Show how to glue the markers to the corners of the envelopes.
3. Instruct the students to cut around the marker shape, through both sides of the envelope, to make a "pocket."
4. Have the class look up prayer scriptures in their Bibles and use their Prayer Markers to mark the pages they select.

Note: Used envelopes work well for this craft.

Miscellaneous Projects of Prayer

Partners in Prayer

bulletin board

· · · · · · · · · · ·

Materials

• pattern, duplicated
• lettering (see below)
• pictures of missionaries
• construction paper
• picture of each child

Directions

1. Cover the bulletin board with the paper of your choice.
2. Cut out lettering for "Partners In Prayer" and "Pray for each other. James 5:16." Place "Partners in Prayer" in an arch shape at the top of the board.
3. Post the James 5:16 verse in an arch at the bottom of the bulletin board.
4. Cut half-circles from construction paper and attach for the border. Write "We are praying for you" on the half-circles (one letter per half).
5. Attach pictures and information about missionaries to the middle. Display a different missionary each week.
6. Cut out the PIP circles and glue the children's pictures to the backs. Place them around the middle picture.

Miscellaneous Projects of Prayer

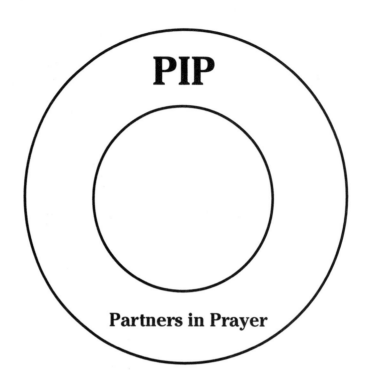

finished bulletin board

Private Prayer Time

Materials
- door hanger, duplicated
- praying hands stickers
- scissors

Directions
1. Have the students color and cut out the door hanger. Provide stickers for decorating.
2. Instruct the class to cut the hanger at the open line and cut out the hole.
3. Tell the students to place the hangers on their doorknob at home when having prayer time so they won't be disturbed.

Discuss
Say, **How often should we pray? Is it important for us to pray each day? What happens if you are in the middle of your prayer time and you are interrupted?**

Pray for each other.
James 5:16

Wiggle Buster
for Little Pray-ers

Directions

Sing to the tune of "This Is the Way I Wash My Clothes." Teach the children the motions first, then lead the song. Then, have them put the motions and the song together. After everyone knows the song well, begin speeding it up as you go through it again and again until the class cannot move any faster!

I bow my head
> *drop chin to chest*
and bend my knees,
> *deep knee bend*
bend my knees,
> *deep knee bend*
bend my knees.
> *deep knee bend*
I bow my head
> *drop chin to chest*
and bend my knees,
> *deep knee bend*
to pray to Jesus Christ.
> *kneeling, folded hands*

I pray when I am riding my bike
> *hands holding to bike*
> *handles, walk around room*
> riding my bike,
> riding my bike.
I pray when I am riding my bike,
> and Jesus hears me.

I pray when I am jumping rope,
> *arms flipping rope while jumping*
jumping rope,
jumping rope.
I pray when I am jumping rope,
and Jesus hears me.

Wherever I go or whatever I do,
> whatever I do,
> whatever I do.
Wherever I go or whatever I do,
> Jesus hears me pray.

Musical Prayers

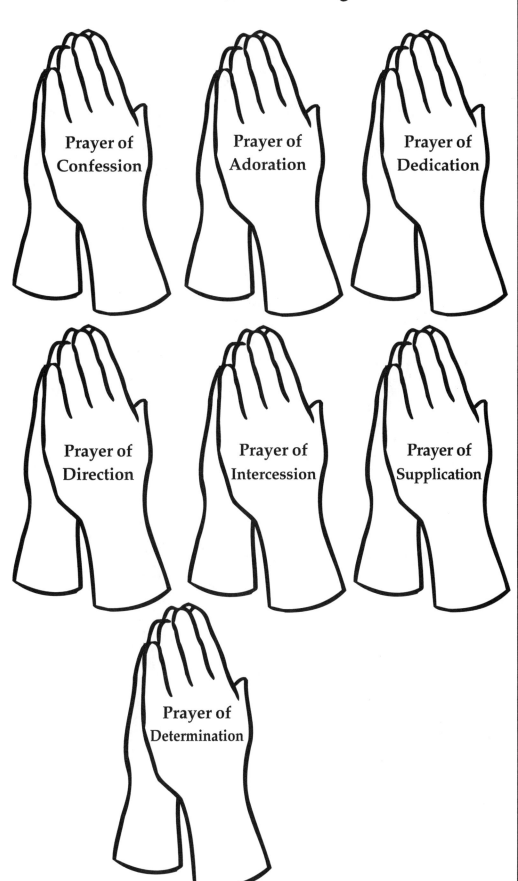

Prayer of
Confession

Prayer of
Adoration

Prayer of
Dedication

Prayer of
Direction

Prayer of
Intercession

Prayer of
Supplication

Prayer of
Determination

game

Materials
- praying hands, duplicated
- chairs
- scissors
- tape
- tape recorder and music cassette

Directions
1. Place chairs in a circle.
2. Cut out the praying hands and tape one to each chair.
3. Have the children circle the chairs while the music plays.
4. When the music stops, each child should find a chair to sit in.
5. Call out a prayer theme (i.e.; determination, adoration).
6. The child sitting in that chair stands and recites the memory verse.
7. Repeat until all of the verses have been reviewed.

Miscellaneous Projects of Prayer

activity

Materials
- prayer board and hands, duplicated from pp. 94-95
- clear, self-stick plastic
- scissors
- marker or pen

Directions
1. Write each class member's name on the prayer board (make more than one if necessary), including teachers.
2. Cut out the praying hands and put the same names on them.
3. Cover the board and hands with clear paper.
4. Each week, place a different praying hands piece on a different square.
5. Instruct the children to pray for the person in their square.
6. Allow the class to share their prayer requests.

Variation
Fill the blocks with missionary names, pastor, organist, etc.

Praying for Each Other

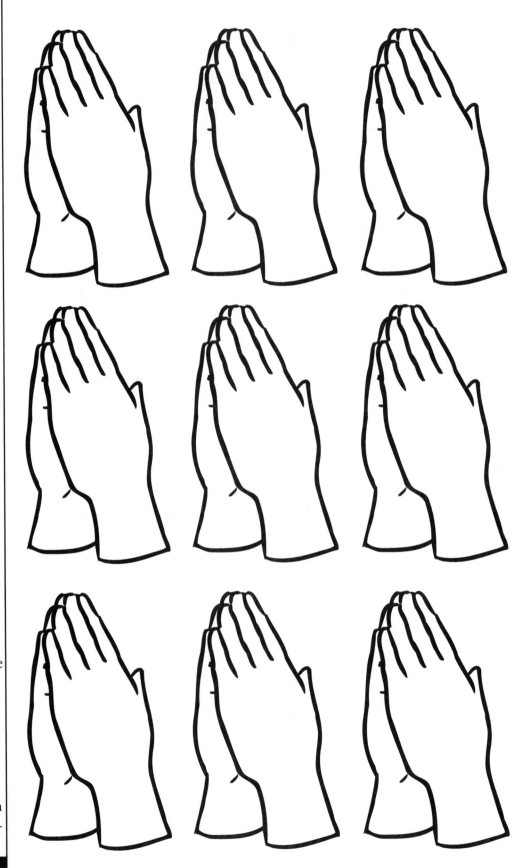

Answers to Puzzles

Selfish or Unselfish, p. 11
selfish: ball glove; make teacher;
unselfish: sunshine; Mary; show me; thank you;
    sister; help me
praise: sunshine; thank you

Missing Memory Verse, p. 18
confess, Lord, forgave, guilt, sin
mystery word: CONFESSION

Sinful Hearts, p. 21
1. stealing
2. lying
3. cheating
4. unkindness
5. unforgiveness
6. disobedience

Leaving the Pigs, p. 24
pigs: I am sorry
posts: You are forgiven

Vowels of Praise, p. 32
I will praise you, O Lord, with all my heart.
Psalm 9:1

Look It Up, p. 41
Jesus, Olives, disciples, cup, yours, Jesus

Following Jesus, p. 50

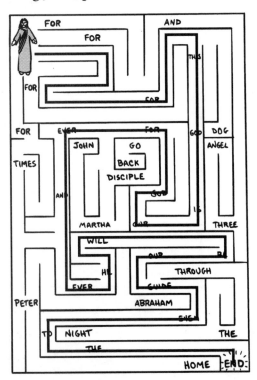

Friends, p. 51
S, E, J, S, U; Jesus

Friendship Praying, p. 58
Pray for each other…The prayer of a righteous
man is powerful and effective. James 5:16

Trouble in the Palace, p. 60
The following things are wrong:
1. Nehemiah on roller skates.
2. Baseball cap on King Artaxerxes' head.
3. Bicycle parked by throne.
4. Ceiling fan.
5. Camel sleeping on rug.
6. Golf club in King's hand.
7. Car showing out of window.
8. King wearing tennis shoes.
9. Nehemiah wearing glasses.
10. Children playing hop scotch on floor.

Talking to God, p. 68
x, y, v, p, p, t, s, r, God, h, i

Oops! The Army Is Out of Order, p. 69
3, 7, 5, 2, 4, 6, 1

Jesus Hears Me, p. 71
play, day, away, say , pray

Weapons, p. 73
circled: torch in jar; ram's horn
boxed: praying hands, Bible

Memory Shapes, p. 79
Be joyful in hope, patient in affliction, faithful in
prayer

Bread, Please, p. 82
For everyone who asks receives; he who seeks
finds; and to him who knocks, the door
will be opened. Luke 11:10